PETS' GUIDES

Bunny's Guide to

Caring for Your Rabbit

Anita Ganeri

Raintree

Raintree is an imprint of Capstone Global Library Limited, a company incorporated in England and Wales having its registered office at 7 Pilgrim Street, London, EC4V 6LB – Registered company number: 6695582

To contact Raintree:
Phone: 0845 6044371
Fax: + 44 (0) 1865 312263
Email: myorders@raintreepublishers.co.uk

Outside the UK please telephone +44 1865 312262

Text © Capstone Global Library Limited 2013
First published in hardback in 2013
First published in paperback in 2014
The moral rights of the proprietor have been asserted.

Edited by Daniel Nunn, Rebecca Rissman, and Sian Smith
Designed by Cynthia Della-Rovere
Picture research by Tracy Cummins
Original illustrations © Capstone Global Library Ltd 2013
Illustrated by Rick Peterson
Production by Victoria Fitzgerald
Originated by Capstone Global Library Ltd
Printed and bound in China by South China Printing Company Ltd

ISBN 978 1 4062 5062 6 (hardback)
16 15 14 13 12
10 9 8 7 6 5 4 3 2 1

ISBN 978 1 4062 5069 5 (paperback)
17 16 15 14 13
10 9 8 7 6 5 4 3 2 1

British Library Cataloguing in Publication Data
Ganeri, Anita, 1961-
  Bunny's guide to caring for your rabbit. – (Pets' guides)
  1. Rabbits–Juvenile literature.
  I. Title II. Series
  636.9'322-dc23

Acknowledgements
The author and publisher are grateful to the following for permission to reproduce copyright material: Capstone Library pp. 7, 11 (Karon Dubke), 17 left, 19, 21 (Tudor Photography); Corbis pp. 15 (© amanaimages), 27 (© Jutta Klee/ableimages); iStockphoto p. 9 (© christopherarndt); Shutterstock pp. 5 (© Cora Mueller), 25 (© foto Arts); Superstock p. 13 (© imagebroker.net); Ros Lamb pp.17 right, p23 (Kween Betty Winzer).

Cover photograph of a Lop-eared baby rabbit reproduced with permission of Getty Images (Geoff du Feu). Design elements reproduced with permission of Shutterstock (© Picsfive) and Shutterstock (© R-studio).

We would like to thank Ros Lamb, Rae Todd, and the team at the Rabbit Welfare Association & Fund for their assistance in the preparation of this book. Further information from the RWAF can be found at: http://www.rabbitwelfare.co.uk

Contents

Some words are shown in bold, **like this**. You can find out what they mean by looking in the glossary.

Do you want a pet rabbit?

Hi! I'm Bunny the rabbit, and this book is all about rabbits just like me! Did you know that rabbits make great pets? We are lively and friendly. But you need to give us lots of care and attention.

Being a good pet owner means making sure that I've got food, water, and somewhere clean and safe to live. Then I'll quickly become your best friend.

Choosing your rabbit

We rabbits come in all shapes and sizes, from giant to quite small. Our coats can be black, white, brown, grey, or a mixture of any of these colours.

Animal shelters often have rabbits that need a good home. You can also buy rabbits from rabbit **breeders** or from good pet shops.

A healthy rabbit

Pick a rabbit that looks active and healthy. It should have clean teeth that are not too long, a shiny coat, clean ears, and bright eyes – just like me!

Rabbits get lonely if we live on our own so please get me a friend. It's best to keep a pair of rabbits together. They should both be **neutered**. Otherwise, you may end up with lots of baby rabbits to look after, too.

Getting ready

Before you bring me home, there are a few things that you need to get ready. This will help to make me feel safer and happier when I arrive. Here is my ready-made rabbit shopping list…

Bunny's shopping list

- a large rabbit house
- shredded paper or hay for bedding
- newspaper and wood shavings for the floor
- a **drip-feeder** water bottle and food bowls
- rabbit food and rabbit toys
- a large **run** that I can play in.

My new home

Rabbits like me need a large house with a living room, a bedroom, and a **run** to play in. Shredded paper or hay makes a cosy bed. I also need a separate place where I can go to the toilet.

Put my house somewhere dry and away from **draughts**. I can live indoors or outdoors. If I live outdoors, make sure you make my home warm in winter. Otherwise, I'll be f-f-freezing cold.

Home, sweet home!

It's time for you to take me home! Use a strong, plastic carrier, with holes in it so that I can breathe. Then put me in my new house and leave me to explore for a while.

I like being stroked but I don't really like to be picked up. Always ask an adult to pick me up for you. They should put one hand under my chest and the other around my bottom, then lift me up. If I start to struggle, put me down gently!

Dinner time

I've had a good look round my new house and now I'm hungry! To stay healthy, I need to eat lots of hay and grass with some juicy dandelion leaves. I need a few good quality **pellets** every day, too.

pellets

Bunny's top meal-time tips

- Make sure that I always have hay and clean drinking water.
- Check which plants you give me. Some plants make me ill.
- Only give me small bits of carrot or fruit as a treat.

Time for play

Like all rabbits, I'm very active and need lots of exercise. Otherwise, I'll soon get bored. A large, fenced-in **run** in the garden is the ideal place for me to hop around and explore.
I should be able to use it whenever I want to.

The run needs a strong wire mesh fence and roof so that I can't escape and cats and foxes can't get in. Add some logs and tubes for me to explore and a sand pit for me to dig in.

Cleaning my house

Nobody likes a dirty home, so please keep my house clean. Every day, take away wet bedding and droppings, and wash out my food bowls and water bottle.

Clean out my whole house once or twice a week. Then, every few weeks, wash it out with warm, soapy water. Don't forget to wash your hands afterwards.

Fur and teeth

To keep my fur clean, I groom it with my paws, but you can help by brushing me once a week. If your rabbit has long hair, brush it every day to stop its fur getting tangled.

Why do rabbits have such long front teeth?
It's because they grow all the time. If they
get too long, I can't eat, so make sure that
I've got plenty of hay and grass to chew on.
This will help to keep my teeth short.

Visiting the vet

If I go off my food, have a runny nose or eyes, or a dirty bottom, I might not be very well. Please take me to the vet at once. The vet will examine me and find out what's wrong.

I also need a check-up twice a year. The vet
will give me **vaccinations** to stop me getting
nasty diseases. You can also get some drops
to put on my fur to stop me getting **fleas**
or **mites**.

Holiday care

You can't take me with you on holiday. If someone else comes to look after me, make sure they have experience in caring for rabbits properly.

If you don't know anyone like this who can take care of me, you should find me a **boarding home** to stay in while you are away. Make sure they are used to keeping rabbits so that I can enjoy my holidays, too.

Rabbit facts

- Wild rabbits live in large groups. They dig lots of underground burrows and tunnels, called **warrens**. Fifty or more rabbits can live in a warren.

- Rabbits have long, strong back legs. They stand up to look out for **predators** and thump their feet on the ground to warn others of danger.

- The Flemish giant is the biggest pet rabbit. It can weigh around 8 kilograms and is about the size of a small dog.

- Rabbits have to eat some of their own droppings, to help them digest the tough grass and hay that they eat.

Helpful tips

- Make sure that your rabbit is picked up and handled from an early age. This helps your pet to get used to human contact and not feel scared.

- If you keep two or more rabbits, make sure that each one has a place to go to get away from the others. Otherwise, they may get unhappy and ill.

- Rabbits love digging. Make sure that your pet has somewhere to dig, such as a digging box filled with earth or child-friendly sand.

- A change in your rabbit's usual behaviour may mean that he or she is not very well. If you are worried, take your rabbit to the vet.

Glossary

boarding home a place where you can leave your pet when you go on holiday

breeders people who have rabbits that need new homes

draughts blasts of cold air that come through a window or under a door

drip-feeder a bottle that is fixed to a rabbit's cage and lets water slowly drip out

fleas tiny insects that can live on a rabbit's skin and fur

mites tiny creatures that can live on a rabbit's fur and inside its ears

neutered when a rabbit has an operation, which means it cannot have babies

pellets small lumps of food

predators animals that hunt and eat others for food

run an outside space where a rabbit can run and hop about

vaccinations medicines given by a vet through a needle to stop rabbits catching diseases

warrens underground burrows and tunnels that wild rabbits live in

Find out more

Books to read

Looking after your Pet: Rabbit, Clare Hibbert (Wayland, 2007)

Rabbits (Pets Plus), Sally Morgan (Franklin Watts, 2012)

Websites

www.rabbitwelfare.co.uk
On this website, you can find a guide to help you learn how to look after a rabbit properly.

www.rspca.org.uk
This is the website of the Royal Society for the Prevention of Cruelty to Animals in Britain. It has lots of information about pet care.

www.thebrc.org
On the British Rabbit Council's website, you can find information about keeping and caring for rabbits, and the history of rabbits as pets.

Index